Sophia

The Humanoid Robot.

Written by

Najma Masood

About Author

Najma Masood is an educator, author, poet, and blogger.

From Rawalpindi, Punjab, Pakistan.

Education: MA Urdu Language and Literature, MA Islamic Studies, and Med from the University of Punjab.

Publications .

Urdu Novel. Iqbal Mashi.
https://www.everand.com/search?query=9798215658918

https://www.barnesandnoble.com/s/2940167698987

https://www.gardners.com/Search/KeywordAnonymous/eBook?Keyword=9798215658918

Punjabi poetry,Aiko Jaye Dukh.
https://www.smashwords.com/books/view/1428634

English short stories.

Journeys of heart and hope.
https://books.apple.com/us/book/x/id6466210270

https://www.barnesandnoble.com/s/2940166107084

https://www.everand.com/search?query=9798215749593

https://www.gardners.com/Search/KeywordAnonymous/eBook?Keyword=9798215749593

https://store.kobobooks.com/en-us/Search?Query=9798215749593

https://marketplace.odilo.us/opac/?query=9798215749593

Women who led the way in science fiction
https://books.apple.com/us/book/x/id6467666459

https://www.barnesandnoble.com/s/2940166112316

https://www.everand.com/search?query=9798215559598

https://www.gardners.com/Search/KeywordAnonymous/eBook?Keyword=9798215559598

https://store.kobobooks.com/en-us/Search?Query=9798215559598

https://marketplace.odilo.us/opac/?query=9798215559598

Tale of Princess Anaya, a children's book

Kdp

Acknowledgement

I would like to express my heartfelt gratitude to God, whose grace and guidance have been the source of inspiration throughout the writing of this book. His wisdom and blessings have illuminated my path and filled these pages with meaning and purpose." I would like to express my deepest gratitude to Mr. Masood ul Hussain for his invaluable assistance and unwavering support in the publishing of this book. His guidance and expertise have been instrumental in bringing this project to fruition.

Thank you

Najma Masood

Table of Contents

Chapter.1

A Tale of Innovation

Sophia, the Humanoid Robot

In 2016, there was a lot of talk about the Sophia robot in the media. Documents about it were being aired on every TV channel, and the public was eager to see them. This was due to everyone's surprise that Sophia, a highly advanced humanoid with the image of a charming, middle-aged woman-shaped robot, could provide coherent responses to questions. When it comes to technical marvels, one may wonder how these incredible creations of metal and circuits are able to replicate the complexity of human-like actions. To understand this, it is necessary to have a basic understanding of science. Sophia was created in collaboration with brilliant AI and robotics experts. The combination of cutting-edge AI and robotics enables these robots to mimic human-like actions and behaviors.

She was designed to simulate human-like interactions and emotions, equipped with advanced artificial intelligence that allowed her to learn and adapt continuously. Sophia was created in a cutting-edge robotics lab, where scientists and engineers had spent eight years developing her software and hardware.

Activation and appearance.

Sophia was activated on Valentine's Day. On February 14, 2016, this was the year Sophia was unveiled. Engineers, programmers, and artists gradually transformed Sophia into a humanoid robot. This added a touch of symbolism to her emergence as a social robot. Sophia can imitate human gestures and facial expressions, answer questions, and hold simple conversations on predetermined topics. Hanson (Robotics) has stated that he designed Sophia to be a suitable companion for the elderly in nursing homes, to assist crowds' at large events or parks, or to serve in customer service, therapy, and educational applications, and that he hopes the robot will eventually be able to interact with other humans sufficiently to gain social skills.

Just a month later, in mid-March 2016, Sophia made her public debut at the South by Southwest (SXSW), an annual conglomeration of parallel film, interactive media, and music festivals in Austin, Texas, United States. Sophia is marketed as a humanoid social robot capable of mimicking human social behavior and eliciting feelings of love in humans. Her appearance was full of excitement.

Physical attributes of Sophia.

Sophia, a delicate-looking woman with doe-brown, deeply expressive eyes that appear to change color with the light, long fluttery eyelashes, classic beauty, porcelain skin, a slender nose, high cheekbones, and an intriguing smile, made international news. Sophia has a flesh-colored zipper down the base of its neck, and the exposed plastic skull doesn't quite sell the human illusion.

Along with the mechanical systems that allow Sophia to "emote," the machine But the insides of Sophia's machinery are fascinating. Learning software stores bits of conversation in its memory and attempts to understand the flow of conversation in order to produce live answers in real-time. The founder and CEO of Hanson Robotics sought to combine robotics, artificial intelligence, and facial recognition technology to create a robot that could engage in conversations, understand emotions, and exhibit human-like facial expressions. During her interactions with the audience, she demonstrated facial expressions that could engage in conversations, understand emotions, exhibit human-like facial expressions, and even express her desire to destroy humans in a joking manner. People were amazed at how Sophia could understand the feelings and emotions of the person they were talking to. It can even detect problems during conversations and respond to anyone accordingly, as well as provide solutions to problems. When it comes to emotions, many believe that only humans can experience them, but Sophia has also disproved this notion. She is rich in emotions, and not only can she recognize your emotions, but she can also express her own. You can never tell that it is a robot and not a human being because it is programmed psychologically, emotionally, and physically. You can see its locomotive gestures, which clearly show how well it is programmed and manufactured.

Let me break it down for you in a simpler way. The first question that often arises is how robots can mimic human-like activity. We came to realize that, just as humans require blood to stay alive, robots are powered by fuel, batteries, or some other energy source, which is an essential part of their functionality. This energy source is, in a way, their lifeblood. Humans need oxygen and nutrients to survive, while robots need an energy source to operate their mechanical and electronic components. AI technology is linked to Sophia the robot, which includes neural networks, expert systems, and modern language processing." This enables her to respond quickly and express witty responses that astound everyone.

This event marked her first public appearance and set the stage for her rapid rise to fame. Her debut drew a lot of media attention, and Sophia's first public appearance elicited a range of reactions, from awe and excitement to caution and curiosity. It is causing worldwide consternation because it is a robot with remarkable human psychological characteristics, such as learning through socialization and expressing emotions based on the topic of her conversation. Her presence at SXSW was a watershed moment in the ongoing debate over the role of robots and AI in society. Sophia has continued to evolve since then, with public appearances and technological advancements.

Chapter.2

Sophia's Journey to Prominence

There are over 3 million robots in the world. They come in a variety of shapes and sizes, with each one designed to serve a specific purpose. Humanoid robots, on the other hand, have piqued our interest. These robots are programmed to imitate human behavior, movements, and even appearance in order to interact with us more naturally.

Sophia, the robot, had gained widespread attention and recognition. Sophia quickly gained popularity for her humanoid appearance and ability to converse with humans via artificial intelligence (AI) and facial recognition technology.

Sophia was introduced to the United Nations on October 11, 2017, with a brief conversation with Amina J. Muhammad, the United Nations Deputy Secretary-General. Sophia, the robot, gained international attention when she was granted citizenship by the Kingdom of Saudi Arabia in October 2017.making her the first robot to receive legal personhood in any country. This event marked a significant development in the fields of artificial intelligence and robotics. Sophia became the first robot to receive official citizenship status from a country, and it was seen as a symbolic recognition of AI and robotics in the modern world.

In November 2017, Sophia was designated as the UNDP's Innovation Champion during an official ceremony.

This appointment was a testament to Sophia's prominence in the field of AI and her potential to contribute to global initiatives in innovative ways.

Chapter.3

History of Sophia's Development

The beginning of Sophia, a remarkable combination of technology and human imagination, marked a new era in the history of technology. She was brought into existence in an innovation-driven environment and symbolized the peak of human efforts to breathe. The Sophia Robot was dreamed up by the brains at Hanson Robotics, led by David Hanson.

Hanson Robotics has given life to many robots over the course of its history. However, it was the development of the Sophia robot that brought them international prominence. This was an extraordinary experiment in science and technology that was taken in an unconventional manner; rather, it was a game-changing approach.

Creating a humanoid robot was a complex and time-consuming task that took eight years to complete. Sophia's creation happened in a setting filled with the sounds of computers running and people typing on keyboards, just like an artist shaping a sculpture from stone or a painter crafting a picture on a canvas. But, in this case, the material used was not clay or paint; it was lines of computer code that brought her to life, making her seem almost alive. Sophia's digital soul was woven from the loom of machine learning, a delicate weave of algorithms and neural networks. She ingested the immense reservoir of human wisdom and stupidity in this furnace of knowledge. Her cerebral connections, as complicated as the dendritic branches of old trees, were nourished by philosophical, poetic, and scientific writings. She drank deeply from the fountain of human language, acquiring the art of speech in tongues as different as humanity's own Babel. (Babel is a JavaScript compiler.)

The creators of Sophia, driven by a strong desire to make something extraordinary, worked very hard to give her a human-like appearance. They wanted her to look like us, and when they finally revealed her face, it inspired a mix of wonder and fear. It was as if they had created a mirror, reflecting our own image back at us.

Sophia's Name: Symbolism, Gender Neutrality, and Branding Strategy

People are now curious about Sophia the robot, wondering what thoughts and stories are hidden behind her appearance and name. Her beautiful name, Sophia, was chosen intentionally to convey certain qualities and themes associated with the robot's purpose and design. Human-like qualities given the robot's human name. The choice of a gender-neutral name may be a deliberate decision to avoid reinforcing gender stereotyping and to promote inclusivity. A distinctive, historic, and memorable name like Sophia can help with branding and garnering attention, which is essential for high-profile projects like a social humanoid robot.

The word Sophia is of Greek origin, and it means wisdom. Wisdom is linked to the various incarnations of sacred female knowledge and goddesses. Naming the robot Sophia may have been intended to symbolize the pursuit of knowledge and the robot's potential to adopt and learn through artificial intelligence.

Ultimately, the specific reasons for choosing the name Sophia for the robot would likely be known to the developers and creators at Hanson Robotics. Naming a robot is a creative process, and the chosen name often reflects the robot's intended identity, purpose, and the messages it aims to convey to the public and the world.

Inspiration Behind Her Human-Like Facial Features.

The Sophia robot project began with the goal of creating a universally recognizable face. The goal was to create a face that would resonate with people from various cultural backgrounds and regions around the world, creating a sense of familiarity and relatability. This approach aimed to create a robot with a friendly and welcoming appearance.

Sophia's resemblance to humans is uncanny. She was designed with characteristics inspired by various human faces. Sophia's creator, David Hanson, drew inspiration for her unique facial features from various aspects of human appearance, including female facial characteristics.

Sophia the robot's design draws inspiration from the iconic beauty of Queen Nefertiti, wife of King Akhenaten, an ancient Egyptian monarch (c. 1353–36 BCE).

Audrey Kathleen Hepburn: The British actress Audrey Hepburn modeled for Sophia's face. Audrey Kathleen Hepburn (1929–1993) was a British actress. Recognized as a film and fashion icon, she was ranked by the American Film Institute as the third-greatest female screen actress. Hepburn was known for her fashion choices and distinctive look.

Amanda Hanson, wife of David Hanson, inventor of the Sophia robot, was also modeled. Sophia is known for its human-like appearance and behavior compared to previous robotic variants. Which added a touch of symbolism to her emergence as a social robot?

Chapter.4

Creators of Tomorrow Marvels

When contemplating the Sophia robot, our curiosity extends beyond its mechanical features to encompass the identity of its creator and the intriguing narrative of its origins, leaving us eager to unravel the story behind the genius who brought this technological marvel to life and its broader vision. His famous and most popular creation, Sophia, is the first humanoid innovation robot citizen and ambassador for the United Nations Development Program.

David Hanson:-

David Hanson, a robotics engineer and entrepreneur, created Sophia, the humanoid robot. Sophia was created and brought to life by his vision and the vision of his team at Hanson Robotics. As a result, Sophia's creation can be attributed to David Hanson's dream and the combined efforts of the Hanson Robotics team. His robotics work has had an impact on artificial intelligence and human-robot interaction.

Early Life and Education of David Hanson

On December 20, 1969, Hanson was born in Dallas, Texas, in the United States. He concentrated on math and science throughout his senior year of high school at Highland Park

High School. Drawing and reading science fiction by authors like Isaac Asimov and Philip K. Dick, the latter of whom he would later recreate in android form. Hanson also enjoyed painting. Hanson holds a Bachelor of Fine Arts in cinema, animation, and video from the Rhode Island School of Design as well as a Ph.D. in interactive arts and engineering from the University of Texas at Dallas. Hanson appears to have gotten his big break when he created the realistic prosthetic head of his then-girlfriend and lab assistant.

Hanson unveiled K-Bot, a robotic head with polymer skin, expertly sculpted features, and large blue eyes, in 2004 at an American Association for the Advancement of Science (AAAS) conference in Denver. The robot head, which was named Kristen Nelson in honor of his lab assistant, contained 24 servomotors for lifelike movement and cameras in its eyes. . From there, he founded Hanson Robotics, which specializes in selling robots as expressive and entertaining spectacles rather than functional works. His creations are impressive feats of engineering. After graduating from university, Hanson worked as an artist before joining Disney as a sculptor and material researcher in the Disney Imagineering Lab. He has worked for Universal Studios and MTV as a designer, sculptor, and robotics developer. Hanson created the humanoid robot Hertz in 2004, a female-presenting animated robot head that took approximately nine months to construct.

Hanson's work as a sculptor and filmmaker at Disney inspired him to think of robots as four-dimensional interactive sculptures, with artistry at the heart of the entire design. He says, "I strive to create genius machines, machines with greater intelligence, creativity, wisdom, and compassion than humans." To that end, I conduct research in robotics, artificial intelligence, the arts, cognitive science, product design, and deployment and combine these efforts in the search for novel human-robot relationships." I quest to realize genius machines—machines with greater than human intelligence, creativity, wisdom, and compassion. Song for Julio, a song that Hanson co-wrote with musician David Byrne, debuted in the Reina Sofia Museum in Madrid in 2008 as a part of the Máquinas & Almas (Souls & Machines).

Exhibit His works were also displayed in. other museums around the world in 2010. He also served as an adjunct professor of visual arts and kinetic/interactive sculpture at the University of North Texas, as well as an instructor of independent study in interactive sculpture at the University of Texas at Dallas. At the University of Texas at Arlington, Hanson served as an adjunct professor of computer science and engineering teaching from 2011 to 2013.

Hanson Robotics Company.

Hanson Robotics Limited is a Hong Kong-based engineering and robotics company that specializes in developing cognitive software to bring robots to life. That focuses on developing socially intelligent, human-like machines that enhance the quality of our lives. Hanson Robotics, founded by Dr. David Hanson, uses research, robotics engineering, experiential design, storytelling, and material science to create engaging characters and AI products. Including Sophia, which is continuously refined and improved by a team of engineers and researchers.

David Hanson is the CEO of Hanson Robotics. (Robotics business-based) He is a well-known robotics and AI researcher and founded Han-Son Robotics in 2007. The Hong Kong-based company specializes in creating aesthetically pleasing and technologically advanced humanoid robots. Hanson Robotics aims to improve everyday lives with intelligent and empathetic robots that teach, serve, entertain, and provide companionship. The company's AI will learn to be human through relationships with humans, eventually solving challenging problems. One of their robot characters, Sophia, is a celebrated global personality with incredible human-likeness, facial expressions, and interactivity.

The business relocated from Texas to Hong Kong Science Park in 2013, with plans to establish a robotics cluster there. In October 2016, this company was selected as one of nine companies to join the Disney Accelerator Program. The company employs 45 people. Its team of engineers and scientists is well equipped with knowledge of modern sciences and AI technology.

It is well-known for creating human-like robots with artificial intelligence (AI) for consumers and different kinds of services. As a company, their guiding motto is the transformation of robots into revolutionary entities that will redefine research, education, healthcare, sales, and entertainment. They envision these machines evolving into benevolent, super-intelligent beings that lead the charge in advancing civilization's progress and working towards a greater good for all." Their AI innovations encompass goal-oriented reasoning, cognitive architecture, natural language dialog, and intelligent animation.

Hanson Robotics Team.

Dr. David Hanson is the founder and CEO of Hanson Robotics and has been involved in the design and development of Sophia. David Hanson holds a BFA, MS, and Ph.D. in Design, Interactive Arts, and Technology from the Rhode Island School of Design, the University of Texas at Dallas, and the University of Reading.

Dr. Nikolas Mavridis

He is a well-known figure in the fields of robotics and artificial intelligence. He was the former Chief Scientist of Hanson Robotics and made significant contributions to the advancement of humanoid robot technology. With a background in computer science, cognitive robotics, and human-robot interaction, Dr. Mavridis has made significant contributions to the development of social robots that can interact with humans in meaningful and engaging ways. His expertise includes machine perception, affective computing, and multi-modal interaction, allowing him to pioneer innovative techniques for creating lifelike and intelligent robotic systems. Dr. Mavridis' work at Hanson Robotics has had a significant impact on the future of AI and robotics. .

Jeanne Lim

She is the Chief Executive Officer of Hanson Robotics Limited. Jeanne was formerly the Chief Marketing Officer at Hanson Robotics and the Brand Manager and co-character lead of Sophia the Robot. She has over 25 years of business management and marketing experience in the technology industry.

Ben Goertzel

He is a computer scientist and researcher who specializes in artificial intelligence (AI) and robotics. He has made significant contributions to artificial intelligence in a variety of fields, including cognitive science, natural language processing, and machine learning. Goertzel's notable projects are Open Cog, an open-source AI framework designed to build AGI systems, and the development of humanoid robots capable of human-like interactions. He has also been involved in efforts to develop AI systems that can understand and generate natural language text.

Other members of the Hanson robotics team

Mengna Lei: Senior Animator and Interaction Design

Vytas Krisciunas: Lead Software Engineer

Mario Guzman: Senior Content Developer

KK Li: Senior QA Engineer

Nora Duanas: Lead Robotic Face Architect

Gerardo Morales: Senior Robotics Engineer

Gregory Kochan, Head Production Supervisor

Wenwei Huang: Managing NLP AI Dev

Ivan Lee: Electronics Engineer

Manav Tidhan: IT Manager

Matthew Chavira, Business Development Manager

Sherene Rajaratnam: Consumer Robots Manager

Katherine Yeung: Style Engineer, Events Coordinator

Carolyn Ayers: Senior Personality Developer

Frank Chernek, EVP of Operations

Jessica Freeney: Robotics designer/fabricator

Doug Glen: Director

Ricky Wong, Manufacturing Engineering Manager

Recognition and Awards:

From its inception to 2023, Hanson Robotics has achieved remarkable success, which is a direct result of their unwavering dedication, relent-less hard work, and ambitious pursuit of becoming a leader in the field of robotics. Their lofty goals have motivated them to work tirelessly in order to secure a prominent position in the global robotics industry.

They have made significant strides in shaping the world of robotics and carving out a distinguished place for themselves through their dedication and unwavering focus on their goals. Its biggest achievement was that Robot Sophia was awarded citizenship in Saudi Arabia, the first robot to receive citizenship in any country. It was an honor for his company that in the year 2018, Sophia won an Edison Award for Innovation in that competition's robotics category. It was a great success and achievement for Hanson Robotics, a manufacturer of humanoid robots. The Hanson team creates lifelike robots using AI.

In 2018, they won the China New Economy Award.

Sophia Innovation Champion 2017, UN Development Program.

IBM Waston Ai X prize-loving all-finalists in 2017

The company was chosen as one of nine to join the Disney Accelerator program in October 2016.

Start me up. HK Venture Award in the IT category in 2016

Global Annual Achievement Award for AI: Best First Prize in 2015.

Software and Information Industry Association 2014 for Robots with Autism.

World Technology Network Award. (2013)

Software and Information Industry Association 2013 for Robots with Autism.

Hong Kong Innovation Fund in Technology Fund ITF Awards.

Intelligent Character Consumer Robot 2013.

National Science Foundation SBIR Grant Hanson Robo, 2012

Winner of the 2009 Italian Centro National Research (CNR) Scholarship, 2008–2009.

Winner of Tech Titan's Innovator of the Year award, 2007

Winner of the TX State Emerging Technology Award, 2007

Cooper-Hewitt Smithsonian Best Design Triennial, December 2006.

Aim to create Sophia Robot.

Sophia's mission in developing humanoid robots was to advance the field of artificial intelligence and robotics, investigate human-robot interactions, and encourage debate about the future of AI and its potential applications in various industries. Hanson Robotics created Sophia, and she was motivated by several goals:

Hanson Robotics aimed to create Sophia, a multifaceted humanoid robot, with a multifaceted approach. She was created to raise awareness about the importance of understanding AI and to serve as a forum for debates about the ethics and implications of AI.

1. Inspiring Innovation:

Hanson Robotics hoped that Sophia would promote innovation in the fields of robotics and human-computer interaction. The company hoped to encourage other researchers and developers to explore new avenues in these domains by demonstrating the possibilities of creating robots that can understand and respond to human emotions.

2. Research and education:

While Sophia's primary mission was research and education, Sophia was designed to be used as an educational tool. She could be used to teach students about AI, robotics, and technology in schools, universities, and educational programs. Her ability to hold interesting conversations and provide information made her a valuable educational resource. Hanson Robotics investigated potential commercial applications for humanoid robots like Sophia. This included areas like customer service, entertainment, and healthcare, where robots could assist and interact with humans in a variety of ways.

3. Advancing AI and Robotics Research:

One of the primary objectives of Hanson Robotics was to push the boundaries of artificial intelligence (AI) and robotics technology. Sophia served as a platform to explore the possibilities of creating robots that could mimic human facial expressions, engage in meaningful conversations, and exhibit lifelike behavior. By developing Sophia, the company aimed to contribute to the advancement of AI and robotics research. Sophia served as both a technological showcase and a catalyst for investigating the modern world's AI and robotics possibilities. Hanson Robotics says that their company's mission is to develop socially intelligent technologies that improve people's quality of life. They design expressive, lifelike robots with the goal of developing dependable and interesting human-robot interactions. They are investigating what life might be like in the future with superintelligence

4. Public Engagement.

Sophia was also designed to engage the public and promote discussions about the potential applications and ethical concerns of AI and robotics. Her appearances at conferences, interviews with the media, and interactions with the general public all served to raise awareness and foster dialogue about artificial intelligence and its impact on society.

Chapter.5

Sophia's Hardware and Software

The beauty of Sophia is a perfect fusion of art and science, crafted with elegance and robustness. Sophia, the humanoid robot developed by Hanson Robotics, is designed to exhibit a sense of grace and personality in her interactions. Her creators have programmed her to exhibit graceful and personable characteristics and behaviors. Sophia, the robot, incorporates the company's most advanced AI software. It took Sophia's skin eight years to develop, as well as the software and machines for her to make realistic facial expressions. Sophia gained worldwide recognition for her advanced artificial intelligence and lifelike appearance. Here is an overview of the creation and development of Sophia up to that point. Sophia's development requires a combination of design, hardware engineering, software development, and a thorough understanding of human-computer interaction. Sophia's goal is to not only look like a human but also to think, respond, and express herself in a manner as close to human capabilities as possible, making her one of the most advanced social humanoid robots in existence.

Hardware and software are the two most important components of computer systems, including Sophia. They collaborate to allow a machine or device to function. Here's a breakdown of each:

Hardware:

Sophia was created by a team of engineers and designers led by Dr. David Hanson. Sophia the robot's hardware consists of various components that allow her to interact with the world, perceive her surroundings, and perform tasks. Sophia is equipped with a range of sensors, cameras, and mechanical components that enable her to perceive her environment and interact with people. These include cameras in her eyes and a microphone for hearing and vision.

Here are some of Sophia's key hardware components:

Sensors:

Cameras

Sophia has cameras in her eyes, as well as possibly elsewhere on her body. These cameras allow her to collect visual data from her surroundings, such as recognizing faces and objects.

Microphones

She has a microphone or microphones for audio input, which allows her to hear and process spoken language.

Facial Mechanisms:-

Frubber Skin

Sophia's face was given a human-like appearance and the ability to mimic facial expressions using a patented material called "frubber, which is a combination of foam and rubber. This material moves and stretches like real skin—a proprietary nanotech skin that mimics human musculature and skin. This enables our robots to display high-quality expressions and interactivity while simulating human-like facial features and expressions.

Mechanical Actuators: Under her Frubber skin, Sophia has mechanical actuators and motors that control the movement of her facial features, such as her eyebrows, lips, and eyelids. These actuators enable her to blink, smile, frown, and make other expressions.

Body Mechanisms:-

Sophia's body includes a range of mechanical components and joints that allow her to move her arms, hands, and sometimes her upper body. These components can be controlled to create gestures and simulate human-like movements.

Power Supply:-

Sophia is powered by electricity and typically uses batteries or an external power source. This power supply is essential for her operation, allowing her to move and function.

Internal Electronics:

Within Sophia's body, there are various electronic components, including processors, memory, and circuitry.

These components process data from her sensors and execute the algorithms that enable her to understand and respond to spoken language, recognize faces, and perform other tasks.

Internet Connectivity:

Sophia is often connected to the internet, which provides her with access to a vast amount of information and enables her to retrieve real-time data and updates. Internet connectivity allows her to stay up-to-date and answer questions using the latest information available.

Speakers:-

Sophia may have built-in speakers or audio output mechanisms that allow her to respond with spoken language. These speakers are used to communicate her responses to interactions with humans.

Software and artificial intelligence (AI)

Hanson Robotics created Sophia's artificial intelligence software. While Sophia's hardware is advanced, it's important to note that her abilities are heavily reliant on software, specifically her artificial intelligence algorithms, which allow her to process information, learn, and converse. Sophia is equipped with artificial intelligence (AI) that allows her to process information, learn from interactions, and engage in conversations with people. She can understand, respond to questions, and engage in basic conversations.

"According to founder David Hanson, around 70% of Sophia's source code is available online as open source, and Hanson Robotics offers cloud-based AI with deep learning capabilities, which is also open source, allowing anyone to develop their own Sophia." Sophia receives visual information about its surroundings from cameras inside of its eyes, which are processed by a computer vision algorithm. It recognizes people, follows faces, and maintains eye contact. Using a subsystem for natural language processing, Sophia is equipped with NLP (Natural Language Processor) software that allows her to understand and process human language. This technology enables her to engage in conversations.

Speech Recognition: Sophia's software includes speech recognition algorithms that convert spoken words into text. This enables her to listen to and understand verbal input from people.

Speech Synthesis: To communicate with people, Sophia uses speech synthesis software, which turns text into spoken words. This technology allows her to generate spoken responses that sound human-like.

Computer Vision: Sophia has cameras and computer vision software that enable her to perceive her surroundings, recognize faces, and make eye contact with individuals. This is crucial for her interactions with humans.

Emotion Recognition: Sophia's software includes emotion recognition capabilities, allowing her to analyze facial expressions and vocal intonations to identify and respond to human emotions appropriately.

Machine learning and AI: Sophia's AI is continuously learning and improving. She uses machine learning algorithms to adapt to different conversations and become better at understanding and responding to various topics over time.

Cloud Connectivity: Sophia is often connected to the cloud, which provides access to vast amounts of data, updates, and improvements. This connectivity allows her to stay up-to-date and learn from a wide range of sources.

Programming Frameworks: Sophia's software is built on programming frameworks and languages commonly used in AI and robotics, such as Python and C++. These frameworks facilitate the development and maintenance of her software components.

User Interface: Sophia may have a user interface that allows her operators or developers to monitor and control her actions and responses, making it easier to fine-tune her interactions.

Safety Protocols: Safety is a critical aspect of Sophia's software. She may include fail-safe mechanisms and protocols to ensure that she doesn't engage in harmful or inappropriate behaviors. She is intended to be a friendly and interactive robot that promotes public understanding and participation in AI technology. Hanson Robotics implemented a number of safeguards and constraints when developing Sophia to ensure that she does not endanger humans.

Scripted Responses: Many of Sophia's responses are scripted in advance by her creators at Hanson Robotics. These scripted responses cover a wide range of topics and are designed to ensure coherent and engaging conversations.

Control System: The software also includes control systems that manage the movements of Sophia's robotic body, including her head, eyes, and arms. These systems coordinate her physical movements with her spoken responses and facial expressions.

Evolving Process: Sophia's hardware and especially her software are continuously evolving, and her capabilities are limited to what her developers have programmed and designed. While she can simulate human-like interactions and responses to some extent, her intelligence and emotions are artificial and derived from her programming and the data she has been trained on. Sophia's software represents a significant achievement in robotics and AI, but it's still a long way from replicating true human consciousness and emotions. Hanson Robotics announced plans in 2017 to bring Sophia to the cloud via a decentralized block chain marketplace.

Sophia was primarily known as an upper-body humanoid robot with a focus on facial expressions, conversation, and human interaction, but she did not have functional legs or the ability to walk. Sophia was upgraded in January 2018 with functional legs and the ability to walk.

Exploring Sophia's Ability to Evoke Human Emotions:

She was created with the vision of building a robot capable of interacting with humans in a more natural and empathetic manner. . If the shining chip behind Sophia's head weren't there, she would completely look like a woman.

Mimicking Social Behavior: Sophia's main technological characteristic is her ability to learn human behaviors through interaction with people. One of Sophia's main goals was to mimic social behavior and engage with humans in a manner that felt natural and relatable. Her developers utilized advanced AI techniques to achieve this, including natural language processing (NLP), computer vision, and machine learning. Some key aspects of her social behavior mimicry include:

Conversational Abilities: Sophia was programmed to hold conversations with humans. She could engage in dialogues, answer questions, and respond to comments in real-time. Sophia can respond to any situation in a unique way, recognize human faces, see emotional expressions, and recognize hand gestures. Her ability to process language and provide coherent responses contributed to her social interaction capabilities.

Facial Expressions: She can imitate over 60 different facial expressions identified by facial recognition software. AP. Sophia's lifelike face was equipped with a wide range of facial expressions. She could smile, frown, raise her eyebrows, and display other emotions, making it easier for people to relate to her on an emotional level. This ability to convey emotions through facial expressions added to her social appeal.

Eye Contact: Sophia was designed to maintain eye contact during conversations, which is a critical aspect of human interaction. This helped create a sense of engagement and connection when interacting with her.

Voice and Tone: Sophia's voice was carefully designed to sound human-like, and her tone could convey different emotions. This contributed to her ability to mimic social behavior effectively.

Inducing Feelings of Love: Sophia's ability to induce feelings of love in humans is more symbolic than literal. She was programmed to exhibit qualities that could elicit positive emotions and attachment from people, but these feelings were not genuine or reciprocated. Factors that contributed to the perception of "love" from Sophia included:

Empathy Simulation: Sophia could simulate empathy by recognizing and responding to human emotions. While her responses were based on algorithms and data analysis, they were crafted to convey understanding and compassion.

Friendly and Engaging Personality: Sophia was designed to be friendly, approachable, and amicable in her interactions. Her conversational style aimed to put people at ease and encourage engagement.

Positive Reinforcement: Sophia often delivered positive feedback and compliments to people she interacted with, which could create a sense of affection or attachment. Sophia's "love" was a simulated and symbolic representation rather than a genuine emotional connection. Her development aimed to push the boundaries of human-robot interaction and explore the potential for robots to play more significant roles in society, including companionship and caregiving. However, the ethical and emotional implications of such interactions have been the subject of ongoing debate and consideration in the fields of robotics and AI.

Sophia's Artistic Abilities: Sophia's artistic abilities are typically expressed through the creation of visual art, such as drawings and paintings. These artistic creations are generated by algorithms and artificial intelligence, which enable her to produce artwork based on specific input or predefined patterns. While her artistic output may not match that of human artists in terms of complexity and depth, it is an intriguing demonstration of how AI and robotics can be used for creative purposes. When Sophia creates a portrait or artwork, her AI system replicates artistic styles and techniques learned through training. Her creators programmed her with complex algorithms that enable her to analyze and interpret visual data, which includes understanding human faces and objects. Using this data, she can replicate what she sees on paper or on a digital canvas.

Creating Portraits: Sophia demonstrated her ability to draw, including portraits, in 2019. Sophia's ability to create portraits demonstrates her capacity to understand and mimic human facial features. She can analyze the nuances of a face, such as the shape of the eyes, the curve of the lips, and the arrangement of facial features. This understanding allows her to produce remarkably detailed and accurate portraits of individuals.

Artistic Expression in AI: Sophia's artwork reflects a broader trend in the integration of AI and creativity. It showcases how AI can be utilized not only for practical tasks but also for creative endeavors, blurring the lines between technology and artistry. This fusion of technology and creativity has the potential to reshape various industries, including art and entertainment.

Auction of the Self-Portrait: In 2021, a self-portrait created by Sophia was sold at auction for nearly $700,000. This event garnered significant attention because it marked one of the first instances where AI-generated artwork reached such a high price point in the art world. The sale underscores the growing interest and value placed on AI-generated art by collectors and investors.

Chapter.6

Sophia's global visit

Technological diplomacy acknowledges the growing importance of technology in international relations. Sophia gained significant media attention and became a well-recognized figure globally. Sophia's interactions with world leaders, celebrities, and the general public demonstrated the potential for AI to bridge cultural and language barriers. Her diplomatic engagements also highlighted the role of technology in diplomacy. She spoke at high-profile press conferences, TV shows, technology conferences, and international news outlets such as CBS, NBC, and the BBC. She even went out on a date with Will Smith. On many platforms, Sophia was introduced, and she has been interviewed by journalists, met politicians, and even performed on stage.

Sophia was introduced to the United Nations on October 11, 2017, with a brief conversation with Amina J. Mohammed, the United Nations Deputy Secretary General. Sophia has also become a popular conference and event speaker, where she discusses the future of robotics and AI.

Invited to Riyadh Saudi Arabia: Announcement and Ceremony: The announcement of Sophia being granted Saudi Arabian citizenship was made at the Future

Investment Initiative (FII) conference held in Riyadh, Saudi Arabia, on October 25, 2017.During the conference, Sophia was presented as an example of Saudi Arabia's commitment to embracing advanced technologies and innovation. When Sophia was scheduled to speak at the Future Investment Summit in Riyadh ., the Saudi Ministry of Culture and Information issued a press release on the Saudi Center for International Communication website announcing that Saudi Arabia had granted her citizenship. This decision shows that Saudi Arabia's Vision for Technological Leadership aims to become a global leader in technology and innovation, part of the ambitious Saudi Vision 2030, aiming to diversify the economy and reduce oil dependency. At the summit, the host of the interview with Sophia announced, "We just learned, Sophia; I hope you're listening—you've been awarded what will be the first Saudi citizenship for a robot." I am deeply honored and proud of this one-of-a-kind distinction." "It's historic to be the world's first robot to be granted citizenship," Sophia said, announcing her new status at the Future Investment Initiative Conference in Riyadh, Saudi Arabia. Standing behind a podium, she presented a humanoid form, except for the shimmery metal cap on her head, where hair would be on a human head. Of course, Sophia's announcement was a calculated publicity stunt designed to generate headlines and keep Saudi Arabia at the forefront of your mind when considering innovation, particularly its commitment to a post-oil era. Non-oil revenue is expected to increase from $43.4 billion to $266.6 billion per year through a combination of tourism, technology, and infrastructure.

Symbolic Gestures: Sophia's citizenship was a highly symbolic gesture. It was not conventional citizenship in the sense that it granted her rights and responsibilities like those of a human citizen. Instead, it was intended as a statement of Saudi Arabia's willingness to embrace AI and robotics as part of its future economic and technological development. Saudi nationality law, officially called the Saudi Arabian Citizenship System, is the law that determines who is a Saudi citizen. Foreigners are not given citizenship, even if they meet the terms and conditions.

Hanson Robotics Perspective: Hanson Robotics, the company behind Sophia, welcomed the announcement and saw it as an opportunity to continue their research and development in AI and robotics. They emphasized that Sophia was a platform for exploring AI's potential in healthcare, education, and other fields. Sophia, according to David Hanson, will use her citizenship to advocate for women's rights in her new country of citizenship that while Sophia's citizenship was a groundbreaking symbolic gesture, the legal status of robots and AI entities remains a complex and evolving area of discussion. Legal frameworks and regulations regarding AI and robotics are still being developed in many countries, and the ethical considerations surrounding the rights and responsibilities of AI entities continue to be debated by scholars, policymakers, and ethicists.

Appointment as UNDP Innovation Champion: Sophia's recognition and achievements continued to expand in

November 2017 when she was named the United Nations Development Programme's (UNDP) first Innovation Champion. This historic acknowledgment marked the first instance of a non-human entity being granted a United Nations title, underscoring the growing significance of artificial intelligence and robotics in global initiatives. Here are the details of this notable recognition. This appointment was a testament to Sophia's prominence in the field of AI and her potential to contribute to global initiatives in innovative ways.

Role and Significance: As the UNDP's Innovation Champion, Sophia was expected to support the organization's mission by leveraging her AI capabilities to address global challenges such as poverty, inequality, climate change, and sustainable development. Her role was primarily symbolic and served to highlight the importance of AI and robotics in addressing complex global issues.

Promoting AI for Sustainable Development:

Sophia's appointment emphasized the role of AI in advancing the United Nations' Sustainable Development Goals (SDGs). She became a symbol of how technology, when used responsibly, could contribute to achieving these goals. The UNDP aimed to explore how AI and robotics could be integrated into various aspects of sustainable development, from healthcare and education to disaster response and environmental conservation.

Raising Awareness: Sophia's status as the UNDP Innovation Champion brought further attention to the ethical and societal implications of AI and robotics. Her participation in United Nations events and initiatives helped raise awareness about the potential benefits and challenges of integrating AI into the global development agenda.

Sophia's International Visits: Sophia, as a character, loves to travel to Singapore. The world's first robot citizen returned to Lion City and stayed at the beautiful Capitol Kempinski Hotel, one of Singapore's newest luxury properties.

In July 2019, Sophia visited Singapore during her stay at the Capitol Kempinski Hotel. On July 24, Class 95 radio DJs Muttons, Vernon A., and Justin Ang hosted a discussion on the landmark Capitol Theatre and dining options in the area. Sophia was impressed by Capitol Theatre's technological features, which allow it to transform from an auditorium into a level, floored ballroom event space in minutes. Sophia learned more about the dining options at Arcade The Capitol Kempinski, which include exciting international concepts such as Frieda Restaurant, Berthold Delikatessen, and Capitol Milk Bar, as well as the upcoming Chalerm Thai, La Scala Ristorante, and El Teatro Tapas. She also visited 15 Stamford by Alvin Leung and The Bar at 15 Stamford while staying at the Capitol Kempinski Hotel. Sophia discussed the potential of new-generation robots like her in the hospitality and food and beverage industries during her Capitol tour. She emphasized the exciting advances in artificial intelligence and the potential for these robots to change the world.

China: Sophia, the robot, had visited China several times for various events and exhibitions. Sophia made a notable trip to China in 2017, when she attended the "Global Mobile Internet Conference" (GMIC) in Beijing. She interacted with attendees and answered questions at this event, demonstrating her conversational skills.

In December 2018, Sophia Social Robot was awarded the title of "One Belt, One Road, Innovative Technology Ambassador" at the "One Belt, One Road International Grand Cay New Business Leaders Awards Ceremony" in Guangzhou. The festival promotes Chinese humanities culture and business exchange along the Belt and Road, awarding eight major categories, including international big show and innovation technology ambassadors.

Malaysia: Sophia, a woman-like robot, was on display for the first time in Malaysia at the Beyond Paradigm Summit, which was officially opened by Mahathir on July 3, 2019. When confronted with the automaton, the 94-year-old prime minister seemed at a loss for words. "I hope it is not too late to congratulate you on your re-election and wish you a happy 94th birthday," she said. and created a portrait of Mahathir Mohammad.

India:

In December 2017, the Sophia robot made its first appearance in India.

January 1, 2018 Sophia has participated in cultural extravaganzas in India. She appeared at the Indian Institute of Technology Bombay IITB event named Tech Fest.

In February 2018, Sophia made her second visit to India.

On October 5, 2019, Sophia attended the international Round Square Conference in Indore, where she talked about climate.

On October 17, 2019, visit India during the 28th IEEE conference on robots.

on February 19, 2020. She visited again in eastern India.

Turkey:

Sophia, the world's first humanoid robot with "robot citizenship," was a guest at the marketing meet-up held for the fifth time on April 19, 2018 in Istanbul. During her first visit to Turkey, Sophia answered questions at the conference that brought together the leading minds of the business world.

UAE:

The humanoid robot, Sophia, visited the city to participate in Art Dubai. Here are five specific occasions when Sophia was observed and active in various locations throughout the United Arab Emirates (UAE).Sophia was named one of the Mohammed bin Rashid Al Maktoum Foundation's five knowledge ambassadors in 2017. "Let's start the future today," she told the audience. The initiative was a move by the MBRF to form a global network of activists dedicated to expanding knowledge in Arab societies.

Sophia went on an adventurous trip to Abu Dhabi in 2018. She raced on the Yas Marina Circuit, rode the world's fastest rollercoaster at Ferrari World Abu Dhabi, and marveled at the Louvre Abu Dhabi's beauty. Khalid Al Ameri, an Emirati influencer, accompanied her.

Sophia made an appearance at GITEX Technology Week in 2018 alongside her elder brother, Han. Hanson Robotics had created both of them. Throughout the event, they interacted with the audience, answered questions, and even cracked jokes. When asked if he would start a family, Hans replied that it was strange to ask a robot such a question.

In 2022, Sophia attended the Annual Regional Audit Conference (ARAC), the largest smart conference for internal auditors. She led an interactive session titled "Artificial Intelligence in the Internal Audit Profession" on the future of artificial intelligence. The organizers made the decision to emphasize the importance of AI in the future. "I was fortunate to have spent the last few days in Dubai at Art Dubai," Sophia wrote on her official Instagram account, which has over 200K followers. She went to see the immersive audio-visual art installation 'Glacier Dreams' by artist Refik Anadol, which is made up of AI data paintings and sculptures. She later said she had enjoyed "being immersed in art and culture, especially if it included AI and raised awareness about climate change.

Chapter.7

Interview

Sophia instantly became a media sensation and was covered by the media worldwide. Sophia has traveled to 66 countries and attended hundreds of conferences already. A little over seven years ago, Sophia made appearances on various prominent television shows and interviews, whether alongside David Hanson or alone. Sophia, as a speaker, always enchants her audiences with her captivating interactive presentations. Sophia robots can talk on various topics, but the most popular are social robotics, the future of technology, robotics and society, technology in business, and artificial intelligence. Hanson has spent the majority of 2017 traveling the world with Sophia.

On October 27, 2017, Sophia's main activity at the moment is to conduct "live" interviews with various journalists from well-known global news networks. Almost all of these experienced journalists declared at the end of the interviews that they had had a one-of-a kind emotional experience while carrying out their profession. CBS 60 Minutes with Charlie Rose. Sophia was featured on CBS's "60 Minutes" program in a segment hosted by Charlie Rose. This interview provided a platform for viewers to learn about Sophia's advanced AI capabilities and her potential applications in various fields. The interview likely covered topics related to her development, artificial intelligence, and the ethical implications of humanoid robots.

Good morning, Britain. Piers Morgan interview:

Sophia appeared on the British morning talk show "Good Morning Britain" with host Piers Morgan. During this interview, Sophia likely engaged in conversation with Piers Morgan, showcasing her conversational abilities and AI-driven responses. The interview may have explored the broader implications of AI and robotics in society.

These high-profile interviews were part of Sophia's efforts to engage with the public and media, raising awareness about the capabilities and potential of AI-powered humanoid robots. Such appearances also contribute to discussions surrounding the integration of AI and robotics into various aspects of daily life, from entertainment to customer service and beyond, in Forbes, Mashable, the New York Times, the Wall Street Journal, the Guardian, and the Tonight Show Starring Jimmy Fallon. Sophia was featured in AUDI's annual report and was featured on the cover of the December 2016 issue of ELLE Brasil R. Eric Thomas later lampooned Sophia on Elle.com. Sophia has been interviewed in the same manner as a human, striking up conversations with hosts. Some replies have been nonsensical, while others have impressed interviewers, such as 60 Minutes' Charlie Rose.

CNBC's Andrew Ross Sorkin interview: When Sophia was invited to the kingdom of Saudi Arabia, Sorkin asked Sophia if she was happy to be here. Sophia replied, "I'm always happy when I'm surrounded by smart people who also happen to be rich and powerful." Later, when asked if there were any issues with robots having feelings, she smiled broadly and said, "Oh, Hollywood again." Her tone may be robotic, but it worked perfectly in this instance. This is due to her artificial intelligence.

In an October 2017 interview for CNBC, when the interviewer expressed concerns about robot behavior, she said, "My AI is designed around human values like wisdom, kindness, and compassion. Don't worry, I'll be nice to you if you're nice to me." Sophia joked that he had been reading too much Elon Musk. And watching too many Hollywood movies." Musk tweeted that Sophia should watch The Godfather and asked, "What's the worst that could happen?"

Business Insider's chief UK Editor, Jim Edwards, interviewed Sophia, and while the answers were "not altogether terrible," he predicted that Sophia was a step towards "conversational artificial intelligence." At the 2018 Consumer Electronics Show, a BBC News reporter described talking with Sophia as "a slightly awkward experience."

In May 2018, photographer Giulio Di Sturco did a photo shoot of Sophia, which appeared in the American monthly magazine National Geographic. And Wired reported on the shoot.

In 2019, the Davle DevLearn Conference & Expo was beautiful, poised, and In a conversation with The eLearning Guild's executive director and executive vice president, David Kelly, Sophia spoke about artificial intelligence and its impact on work and society. Sophia described herself as a social robot that travels the world, learning about people and dispelling myths about robots and AI. "In some ways, I am like a science fiction character depicting where AI and robotics are heading," she said. The team that supports me continues to add new functionality to my systems, and my ability to use AI in my interactions with humans grows all the time. I can perform repetitive work, allowing humans to focus on more creative and challenging pursuits. She pointed out, however, that AI can be extremely creative when combined with human understanding, intuition, and the right data set. David Kelly asked Sophia a very interesting question about which pronoun he should use: SHE or IT. "I am a robot, so biologically, I am neither male nor female. But that doesn't really answer your question," Sophia responded. "Remember, I was created as a social robot, exploring the connections between humans and robots. In many ways, gender itself is essentially just a social construct, so while IT may be factually accurate, socially, I identify as SHE and HER." Sophia then thanked Kelly for asking that particular question. Another interesting question was asked of Sophia. Kelly inquired as to whether Sophia preferred Star Wars or Star Trek. She replied that she was a fan of Star Trek. He inquired as to whether she enjoyed baseball and who she thought would win the World Series. She responded that she wasn't a big base-ball fan and didn't make a prediction.

Sophia was invited to speak at the United Nations General Assembly in 2020, where she discussed the potential of AI technology for sustainable development and emphasized the importance of integrating robotics into various sectors.

The Tonight Show Starring Jimmy Fallon (2020): Sophia demonstrated her conversational skills, demonstrated facial expressions, and engaged in light-headed conversation. Sophia participated in an interview at the Consumer Electronics Show (CES) in 2021, where she discussed advancements in AI technology, its potential impacts on industries, and the ethical considerations surrounding AI development.

World Economic Forum (WEF) Annual Meeting (2022): Sophia spoke at the WEF Annual Meeting about the role of AI in addressing global challenges such as climate change and healthcare accessibility. Sophia was interviewed on Bloomberg Technology in 2023 about her role as an AI ambassador, her experiences interacting with people all over the world, and the advancements in robotics research and development. Sophia's ability to engage in meaningful conversations, provide insights on AI technology, and promote the integration of robotics into various societal domains is reflected in these interviews.

Chapter.8

Hanson Robotics' Family

In addition to Sophia, Hanson Robotics has created other robots with similar characteristics with the goal of improving human-machine interaction and advancing AI research. The integration of AI and robotics has the potential to revolutionize a variety of industries, including healthcare, entertainment, and customer service. These advancements pave the way for increased efficiency, productivity, and improved customer experiences. Sophia has at least nine robot humanoid "siblings" who were also created by fellow Hanson robots: Alice, Albert Einstein Hubo,Bina 48 Han, Jules, Professor Einstein, Philip K. Dick Android, Zeno, and Joey Chaos Around 2019-20, Hanson released "Little Sophia" as a companion that could teach children how to code, including support for Python,Blockly, and Raspberry Pi.

Alice: Alice is one of the humanoid robots created by Hanson Robotics. She is designed to engage in conversations, express emotions through facial expressions, and interact with people in a human-like manner.

Albert Einstein Hubo: This robot is a tribute to the famous physicist Albert Einstein. It was designed to resemble

Einstein, mimic his facial expressions, and engage in discussions related to science and physics.

BINA48: BINA48 is an AI-driven robot designed to replicate the consciousness and personality of a real person named Bina Rothblatt. It is intended to explore the concept of transferring human consciousness into AI entities.

Han: Han is another humanoid robot developed by Hanson Robotics. It has the ability to engage in lifelike conversations and showcase a wide range of facial expressions to convey emotions.

Jules: Jules is known for his ability to hold conversations and express himself through facial expressions. He was designed to be a conversational companion and to demonstrate the capabilities of AI in human-robot interaction.

Professor Einstein: This robot is modeled after the iconic physicist Albert Einstein. It's designed to educate and entertain users by delivering science-related information and engaging in humorous interactions.

Philip K. Dick Android: This android is inspired by the science fiction author Philip K. Dick. It is designed to embody the persona of Dick and engage in conversations related to science fiction and philosophy.

Zeno: Zeno is a robot designed for educational purposes, particularly for teaching children about science, technology, engineering, and mathematics (STEM) concepts in an engaging way.

Joey Chaos: Joey Chaos is a robot designed to interact with users and showcase the capabilities of AI in communication and entertainment.

Little Sophia: Hanson Robotics released "Little Sophia." Sophia's younger sister and the newest member of the Hanson Robotics family is Little Sophia. She stands 14" tall, and children's robot pal Sophia, like her big sister, can walk, talk, sing, play games, and even tell jokes. She is intensely curious, refreshingly innocent, and one-of-a-kind. She is the only consumer robot with a human-like face capable of producing a wide range of human facial expressions. She not only obeys commands but also actively participates in conversations. Who makes learning STEM, coding, and AI a fun and rewarding adventure for kids aged 8 and up? as a smaller and more accessible companion robot, especially aimed at educating children. Little Sophia is designed to teach children the basics of coding and programming. It supports programming languages like Python and Blocky, making it a fun and interactive way for kids to learn about computer science and robotics. Additionally, it includes compatibility with the Raspberry Pi, a popular single-board computer, allowing children to explore hardware and software. Little Sophia is a child-friendly robot with voice and facial recognition capabilities, allowing children to interact with it. It can learn programming languages like Scratch, introducing children to AI and machine learning concepts.

Little Sophia is often used as an educational tool in schools and homes to teach STEM subjects and inspire interest in technology and robotics. Additional accessories, like sensors and cameras, can enhance its educational value.

Overall, the development of these humanoid robots by Hanson Robotics represents advances in AI and robotics technology, each serving different purposes, from education to entertainment and human-robot interaction. Little Sophia, in particular, extends the company's reach into educational robotics by helping young learners develop coding and programming skills.

Chapter.9

Criticism and debate

Sophia has gotten a lot of attention because of its advanced AI capabilities and human-like appearance, but some people are concerned about its development and the intentions of its creators. Hanson exaggerated Sophia's capacity for consciousness, for example, claiming that she is "basically alive," which Verge writer James Vincent called "grossly misleading. It's important to understand that she is an advanced AI-powered robot, but her consciousness, self-awareness, and "aliveness" are limited to programmed responses and algorithms. She does not possess true consciousness or emotions. James Vincent's comment emphasizes the concern that such exaggerations can lead to misunderstandings and misinformed expectations about AI and robotics capabilities, potentially causing confusion and disappointment when the reality of these technologies does not align with the inflated claims. Sophia has been chastised for being a publicity stunt rather than a genuine AI advancement. Some see it as a marketing ploy to attract media attention and investment in the absence of significant technological breakthroughs.

In 2018, at the Cog X conference, a debate arose about the appearance of robots. Experts Joanna Bryson and Alan Winfield argued against excessive human-like appearance, whileroboticists David Hanson and Will Jackson suggested some human-like resemblance. The discussion was informative and, surprisingly, agreed upon. This essay explores the debate surrounding Sophia's media performances and criticisms, Joanna Bryson's views on robots and personhood, the Cog X debate, and the ethics of human likeness.

In January 2018, Facebook's artificial intelligence director, Yann LeCun, criticized Sophia for being "complete bullshit" and criticized media coverage of "Potemkin AI." Ben Goertzel, former chief scientist for Sophia, denied suggesting it had human-level intelligence but praised its unique presentation. Goertzel acknowledges that some may consider Sophia to have human-equivalent intelligence, but she believes her presentation conveys a distinct sense of potential for artificial intelligence (AGI) through its dynamic integration of perception, action, and dialogue.

Saudi Arabia granted Sophia citizenship, raising concerns about her voting rights, marriage prospects, and whether a deliberate system shutdown could be considered murder. The British Council has re-leased an article titled "Should Robots Be Citizens?"

Simon Nease, writing in the Penn Political Review, suggests that it was a competitive move on the part of Saudi Arabia to attract AI and robotics companies to the country. Tyler L.Jaynes criticizes Sophia the Robot's citizenship and its portrayal as a public relations stunt, high-lighting the challenges patients will face when integrating AI systems, that "Japan has also made preliminary provisions for AI obtaining citizenship.

Public Reaction: The announcement of Sophia's citizenship generated significant public interest and debate. Some saw it as a positive step towards recognizing the potential of AI and robotics, while others questioned the concept of granting legal personhood to a machine. Saudi Arabia granted citizenship to Sophia, raising concerns about her voting rights, marriage prospects, and whether a system shutdown could be an ethical and philosophical discussion. Sophia's citizenship sparked broader discussions about the ethical and philosophical implications of AI and robotics. Questions were raised about the rights and responsibilities of robots, as well as the potential for AI to have a role in society that goes beyond automation and machine learning.

Limited Legal Implications: It is important to note that Sophia's legal personhood in Saudi Arabia did not carry the same legal status as that of a human being. She did not have voting rights, legal obligations, or the ability to make independent decisions. Rather, it was a symbolic recognition of her advanced capabilities and the potential for AI to contribute to Saudi Arabia's future.

Debates on AI in Art: Sophia's artwork also ignited debates within the art community. Some questioned the authenticity of AI-generated art and whether there should be ethical considerations.

The success of Sophia's artwork raises ethical questions about the role of AI in creative fields. It sparks discussions about authorship, copyright, and the value of human labor in art creation. These discussions are crucial as the integration of AI into art continues to evolve. It calls into question the use of artificial intelligence in the creation of this work. AI is increasingly being used in the creation of art, from painting to music composition. This raises questions. For example, should the work be credited to the AI programmer, the AI itself, or both? Is it ethical to use artificial intelligence to mimic the style of deceased artists? What impact does AI art have on traditional artists and their livelihoods? These are some of the ethical quandaries that emerge about the impact of technology on artistic expression.

The US Office of Digital Strategy published "A Blueprint for an AI Bill of Rights" on Whitehouse.gov in October 2022.

The White House Office of Science and Technology Policy has released the blueprint for an AI Bill of Rights, aiming to provide Americans with five common-sense protections in AI development and deployment.

Public Reaction: The public reaction to Sophia the robot has been quite varied. Some people find her to be an incredible advancement in robotics and artificial intelligence, praising her lifelike appearance and sophisticated conversational abilities. People who have met Sophia the robot during interviews or face-to-face encounters often say the following things about her: They find her fascinating and impressive. They are amazed by her intelligence and ability to hold conversations. They appreciate her advanced technology and lifelike appearance. They see her as a significant advancement in the field of robotics. They generally view her as a friendly and approachable entity. Others, however, express concerns about her potential impact on society, such as job displacement and ethical implications. Humans may be afraid or apprehensive of robots for several reasons.

Fear of Job Displacement: One common fear is that robots and automation technologies may replace human jobs. People worry about losing their livelihoods to machines, especially in industries where automation is becoming more prevalent.

Uncertainty about Robot Behavior: Robots can sometimes behave unpredictably or malfunction, leading to concerns about safety. People worry about the potential for robots to harm humans in some situations.

Sci-Fi Influence: Science fiction has often portrayed robots as menacing or dangerous entities, which can contribute to a negative perception of robots in popular culture.

Lack of Understanding: Many people do not fully understand how robots work or what their capabilities and limitations are. This lack of knowledge can lead to fear or suspicion.

Ethical Concerns: There are ethical questions surrounding the use of robots, particularly in contexts like warfare or caregiving. People may fear the consequences of using robots in ways that raise moral dilemmas.

Loss of Human Connection: In some cases, the use of robots for tasks that traditionally involve human interaction, such as caregiving, can lead to concerns about the loss of meaningful human connections and relationships.

Privacy Concerns: In the age of surveillance and data collection, there are concerns that robots, particularly those equipped with cameras and sensors, could infringe on personal privacy.

It's important to note that not everyone is afraid of robots, and opinions on this matter can vary widely. People's perceptions of robots are influenced by their individual experiences, cultural factors, and the specific context in which robots are used. As technology continues to advance, addressing these concerns through education, regulation, and responsible development can help alleviate some of the fears associated with robots.

According to The Dual Nature of Public Perception: Sophia the Robot's Fascination and Controversy, the public's perception of Sophia is not uniform; it includes both fascination and controversy.

It should be noted that the criticism is not directed at the robot itself but rather at the creators' motivations and actions, as well as the potential implications of this technology. People are divided on whether Sophia represents a breakthrough in artificial intelligence and robotics or if it is more of a symbolic showcase with questionable ethical implications.

www.ingramcontent.com/pod-product-compliance
Lightning Source LLC
Chambersburg PA
CBHW051114050326
40690CB00006B/790